Disclaimer: The information contained in this book is based on the experience and research of the author. It is not intended as a substitute for consulting with your physician or other health-care provider. Any attempt to diagnose and treat an illness should be done under the direction of a health-care professional. The publisher and author are not responsible for any adverse effects or consequences resulting from the use of any of the suggestions, preparations, or procedures discussed in this book.

Some of the recipes in this book include raw eggs, meat, or fish. When these foods are consumed raw, there is always the risk that bacteria, which is killed by proper cooking, may be present. For this reason, when se1ving these foods raw, always buy certified salmonella -free eggs and the freshest n1eat and fish available fron1a reliable grocer, storing them in the refrigerator until they are se1ved. Because of the health risks associated with the consumption of bacteria that can be present in raw eggs, meat, and fish, these foods should not be consumed by infants, small children, pregnant women, the elderly, or any persons who may be immunocompromised. The author and publisher expressly disclaim responsibility for any adverse effects that may result from the use or application of the recipes and information contained in this book.

CONTENTS

INTRODUCTION

If there is one easy and quick way to consume all the essential nutrients in a single drink, then it is probably from smoothies. These healthy and nutritious drinks are recommended on almost all the health-oriented diet plans due to the rich combination of ingredients they can provide. There are several ways to prepare and enjoy a smoothie. It can be made according to your taste preferences, health needs, and available ingredients. Perhaps, there are endless ways to enjoy a glass of smoothie. In this cookbook, we will discuss all the different ways to prepare healthy and delicious smoothies through amazing smoothie recipes. But before that, let's have a look at some important techniques and tips for making them.

Why Are Smoothies Good for Your Health?

Well, smoothies are healthy because of the combination of the nutrients they can provide in a single serving. Most of the food we eat is cooked or processed, which usually causes the loss of essential nutrients. The fresh, raw, and organic ingredients in the smoothies can provide quality nutrients, and that's what makes smoothies healthy and nourishing.

1. Detox Your Body

One of the biggest health benefits of a smoothie is that it can help detoxify your body and help it get rid of toxins and radicals. It happens due to the antioxidants present in fruits, vegetables, and skins. Normally the smoothies are made out of uncooked and unprocessed ingredients, which ensure maximum intake of antioxidants.

2 Reduce Inflammation

Inflammation is usually caused by the oxidants, toxins, and free radicals circulating in our blood. These toxins can trigger the body's immune system, which results in inflammation in different parts of the body both at cellular or organ level. Smoothies can reduce this inflammation by providing such antioxidants that remove all the toxins from the blood.

3. Healthy Ingredients

According to health experts, an average adult should consume 400 grams of fruits and vegetables per day. But in today's lifestyle, we are more dependent on processed and fast food, and the fresh fruit and vegetable levels are extremely low. Smoothies can help you maintain your fruit and vegetable intake without putting in much effort in cooking and preparation. Moreover, you have the choice to add as many healthy ingredients as possible to meet your nutritional needs.

4. Source of Phytonutrients

Phytonutrients are plant-sourced micronutrients that are commonly present in leafy green vegetables. These phytonutrients can regulate the hormones and enzymes produced in the body, help remove bad cholesterol, prevent cardiac diseases, cause weight loss, and boost metabolic rates. These phytonutrients are often not consumed through a regular diet, but when the vegetables are blended well with fruits in smoothies, more phytonutrients are added to the diet. Thus, smoothies through their high phytonutrient content can help prevent various diseases.

5. Aid Weight Loss

Smoothies only provide clean energy as they are rich in vitamins, minerals, fibers, and phytonutrients; all the macros present in the smoothies are in a very balanced amount. And these nutrients aid the fat burning process by increasing metabolic rates. People who reduce the amount of solid food and start consuming more smoothies live not only a healthy life but also an active one with a perfect body mass index.

6. Improves Digestion

Fibers are responsible for improving the bowel movement in the digestive tract, which then indirectly improves digestion. Smoothies are rich in fiber, which then helps improve digestion. They are also a rich source of macro and micronutrients, which nourishes the friendly gut bacteria living in the human intestines.

7. Lower Cholesterol

The antioxidants and phytonutrients present in the smoothies are responsible for removing the blood cholesterol from the body. They help the body to process these low-density lipoproteins and regulate hormones and enzymes which remove these molecules out of the blood and cleanse it.

8. Increased Fiber Consumption

On average, a human adult must consume 25–38grams of fiber per day. But the food we consume routinely does not offer much fiber. Smoothies, on the other hand, are a rich source of fiber; hence, they can drastically increase the fiber intake of a person and can help him meet his target.

Smoothies: As a Meal Replacement or Just a Snack?

Well, you cannot really replace a complete or full meal with a smoothie as the latter does not provide as many calories as the former. Smoothies can only replace a meal when you are living a special diet with low caloric servings. However, all types of smoothies can easily replace a snack. Snacks are usually consumed in between two meals in order to gain quick energy for a short time. When you replace snacks with smoothies, you don't only get clean energy, but you also get to have a variety of macro and micronutrients due to the different combinations of ingredients used in each smoothie. There are different types of smoothies that you can consume instead of a snack.

1.Fruit Smoothies

These smoothies give you a flavorsome combination of different fruits with milk, cream, water, or superfoods like nuts and seeds. They contain more fiber and carbs. Fruit smoothies are generally more refreshing and delicious.

2.Green Smoothies

These smoothies are known for their rich fiber and phytonutrient content as they are made out of leafy green vegetables. These smoothies are more effective for weight loss. Kale, spinach, parsley, celery, coriander, etc., are usually added to these smoothies along with water, milk, or a cream base.

3.Protein Smoothies

These smoothies are extremely healthy and helpful for those who are looking for a protein-rich diet and working hard to develop strong and healthy body muscles. You can increase the protein content of the smoothies by adding more cheese, cream, eggs, cream cheese, nuts, seeds, and protein powder.

How to Choose Your Blender

Blending is a basic and important step of smoothie making. Without having a quality blender at home, you cannot have a good, smooth, and creamy smoothie to enjoy. That is why a smoothie lover must also know a decent amount about the blender he will need to make those smoothies. While there are tons of blender options out there, you can follow the following standard criterion.

1. Blending Power

The blending powder makes all the difference, there are several low-quality blenders out there that look fancy, but they don't have good blending power. As a result, the smoothie blended in such a blender is not smooth and well mixed. So, you need a blender that has a minimum of 500 watts of power or more. Blenders with this power range can grind and blend all types of vegetables and fruits—whether fresh or frozen—easily. Such blenders are also tough enough to crush solid ice.

2. Size and Material

When it comes to a smoothie blender, the size and material cannot be overlooked. A suitable size of the blender can ensure that you get the perfect amount of smoothie every time. It should be large enough to accommodate all the smoothie ingredients but small enough for you to handle easily. Similarly, the material of the blender jug should be good enough to sustain different cold and warm temperatures, plus the plastic or other materials used in the blender should be food-friendly as well as free from any harmful chemicals or microplastics.

3. Ease and Convenience

While you look for the quality features of a blender, you must also check for the much-needed ease and convenience while buying one. It is important to have a blender jug, which can provide good results with minimum efforts and time. Electric blenders with multiple-sized jugs and ranging blending power are considered most suitable in this regard. These days, you can also find bottle blenders, which are battery-driven portable blenders that can be carried to places. These portable blenders are great for single servings. However, if portability is not the feature you are looking for, then top-shelf blenders are highly recommended.

How to Make a Smoothie

Smoothie making seems simple enough, right? Well, it is! And that's the part which makes a smoothie preferable over other snacks, besides being healthy and nutritious. A smoothie can be prepared in no time by following the given steps:

1. Preparing the Fruits and Vegetables: Frozen or Fresh?

First, you need to prepare the vegetables and fruits according to the recipe of the smoothie. The vegetables and fruits are available in both frozen and fresh forms. Seasonal fruits and veggies that are not always available can be used in their frozen forms. Otherwise, fresh organic fruits and vegetables are preferable. Once you have chosen the form of these ingredients, then prepare them for blending. Remove pits or seeds in the fruits, if possible.

2. Choose a Suitable Base Liquid

Fruits and vegetables alone cannot be blended into a smoothie; you always need a base to blend these ingredients with. You can select the base liquid by analyzing their nutritional values. For instance, if you want a low carb smoothie, then you will use almond or coconut milk instead of animal milk. Or if you want your smoothie to be high in fat, then you will need to add cream or cream cheese to the base. However, water is often added when low caloric smoothies are prepared.

3. Try Different Flavors

In most smoothies, certain additional ingredients are added sometimes to add more flavors or to increase the nutritional values of the smoothie. Different sweeteners are used for flavor like sugar, brown sugar, honey, low-carb stevia, Swerve, erythritol, molasses, powdered honey, etc. Citric juice or other liquids can also be added in this regard. Nuts, seeds, protein powder, matcha powder, chia seeds, green tea liquid, chocolate, cookie crumbs, etc., are other side ingredients that often used in smoothies for good taste and health.

4. Blend! Blend! Blend!

Once all the ingredients are ready for the recipe, the next important step is to bring them together in a blender. You can add everything at once before blending, or if certain ingredients need soaking, then give them a soaking time before blending them with other ingredients. Remember, all smoothies have a creamy, smooth, and thick consistency, so it has to be maintained during blending. The final blended smoothie should come out lump-free.

5. Chill and Serve

Often, ice is crushed with other ingredients of a smoothie to make it chill and cold, but if you have missed that part, then you can refrigerate your smoothie for an hour, at least. When it is chilled well, serve it in suitable serving glasses with your favorite toppings. Choose the smoothie toppings according to the ingredients used in its basic recipe.

Best Superfoods for Smoothies

Superfood is that high energy, nutritious ingredients that can add great nutritional value even when used in smaller quantities. Superfoods are paired with different combinations of fruits and vegetables to fill in the nutritional gaps and provide the dieter all the much-needed nutrients. The commonly used superfoods for smoothies include the following:

1. Hemp Seeds

Go for these little seeds to add a protein boost to your routine smoothies. A three-tablespoon serving of matcha can add ten grams of protein to each serving, which is more than enough to meet your protein needs. In this serving, you can also get ten grams of omega-3 fatty acids, which can support your heart and brain health.

2. Goji Berries

The red-orange berries will definitely add some sweetness to a smoothie. And they also have a number of nutrients as well. They are packed with zeaxanthin, an antioxidant commonly known to improve eyesight and health. Gojis have a good amount of fiber—about 2 ½ grams per two tablespoons of serving.

3. Cacao

Cacao powder, or cocoa powder, are two words that are interchangeably used, but you should know that cacao is the raw, less-processed variety of cocoa, and due to this minimal processing, the cacao is rich in flavonoids. These are the antioxidants that have shown to boost blood flow to the brain. Moreover, cacao also has anti-inflammatory properties.

4. Chia Seeds

Like hemp seed, these small seeds are also packed proteins, omega-3s, and fiber. A two-tablespoon serving can provide six grams of proteins, ten grams of fiber, and five grams of omega 3s. They are also good for meeting your nutritional need for minerals like iron and magnesium.

5.Turmeric

It is a commonly used Indian spice that is added to food for its endless health benefits. The yellow-colored spice can make your drink super healthy and delicious for sure. Turmeric also contains curcumin, which is an anti-inflammatory compound, and the research has suggested that turmeric can also help relieve sore or painful joints.

6.Collagen

You know that collagen is basically a protein that actually supports and promotes good, smooth, and healthy skin. Collagen is largely available in a separate powder form, which is edible and healthy; you can add this powder to your smoothie.

7.Camu Camu

The pale orange powder, Camu Camu, is packed with vitamin C. A single teaspoon of Camu Camu can provide 2,400 milligrams of vitamin C per serving, which is about thirty times more than an orange. That is considered great and healthy for your skin, as vitamin C helps fight against skin damage caused by the UV rays coming from the sun, and it also boosts the production of the skin-smoothing collagen.

8.Maqui

It is a dark purple powder, which provides more of the antioxidants than other fruits like blueberries, acai berries, pomegranates, or blackberries. Maqui is rich in anthocyanins, which a family of phytonutrients that have been seen to have a preventive effect against heart problems and cancer formation. It might help your strength against a common cold or flu; a few pieces of evidence suggest that anthocyanins also have antimicrobial properties.

9.Matcha

If you often visit a coffee shop, then you must be familiar with this matcha green powder. As the matcha powder is a concentrated form of green tea, it is packed with antioxidants like ECGC, which has been used to prevent tumor formation in human cells and reduce the risk for certain types of cancers. Studies have revealed that it has strong anti-infective properties, and it helps boost metabolism in the body.

Common Mistakes to Avoid While Making a Smoothie

Here are some common mistakes that most people commit while making smoothies:

1. Adding More Fruit Than Needed

Remember, fruits are a rich source of sugars and carbs, and some fruits have a high glycemic index like mangoes, watermelon, pineapple, etc. More sugar or carbs are not healthy for people living with health conditions like obesity, diabetes, or insulin resistance. Therefore, it is important to keep the fruit intake balanced and avoid adding an excessive amount of fruit to the smoothie. For instance, add only a handful of berries to a single serving of smoothie or half a cup of other fruits per serving to keep the sugar balanced controlled and maintained.

2. Losing Portion Control

The important part is to keep track of the portion size at the time of each serving. If you are making a smoothie to replace a snack, then it should only contain 6–8 fl. oz., whereas if you are serving a smoothie instead of a meal, then it should be around 10–12 fl. Oz. to provide you all the much-needed calories.

3. Adding More Sugar

Sugar and sweeteners like honey, maple syrup, molasses, etc., may add the desired sweetness to the smoothie, but when you overdo the quantity of sugar in a smoothie, it can drastically increase its carb values, which are hazardous for health. It is better to properly measure out the exact amount of sugar, which is 1–2 teaspoons per serving before adding it to the smoothie. Similarly, add only one date per glass of smoothie. In this way, the sweetness and nutritional values will both be maintained.

4. Overlooking the Dietary Needs

Make sure that you are making your smoothies using all the different food categories. Most people assume that smoothies can only be made out of fruits, which limits their choices. However, there are other groups of food as well from which you can pick and choose your desired ingredients like vegetables, butter, dairy, seeds, and nuts, etc.

5. Longer Storage

Remember that the fruits and vegetables and the milky or creamy base that is used in the smoothie are all perishable food items, which means that they can get spoiled earlier than other items. So, you cannot leave a smoothie in the refrigerator for days. It can only be refrigerated in a closed container for one or two days.

BREAKFAST SMOOTHIES RECIPES

Almond Smoothie

Ingredients

¾ cup almonds, chopped

½ cup heavy cream

2 teaspoons almond butter

¼ teaspoon vanilla extract

7–8 drops liquid stevia

1 cup unsweetened almond milk

¼ cup ice cubes

How to Prepare

1. Add all the ingredients in a high-power blender and pulse until creamy.

2. Pour the smoothie into two glasses and serve immediately.

Preparation time: 10 minutes

Total time: 10 minutes

Servings: 2

Nutritional Values

Calories 364

Total Fat 31.9 g

Saturated Fat 4.3 g

Cholesterol 11 mg

Sodium 111 mg

Total Carbs 13.6 g

Fiber 6.6 g

Sugar 3.5 g

Protein 11.9 g

Banana Oatmeal Smoothie

Ingredients

1½ frozen bananas, peeled and sliced

½ cup old-fashioned oats

2 tablespoons peanut butter

1 tablespoon chia seeds

1½ tablespoons honey

1½ cups unsweetened almond milk

¼ cup ice cubes

How to Prepare

1. Add all the ingredients in a high-power blender and pulse until creamy.

2. Pour the smoothie into two glasses and serve immediately.

Preparation time: 10 minutes

Total time: 10 minutes

Servings: 2

Nutritional Values

Calories 340

Total Fat 13.5 g

Saturated Fat 2.4 g

Cholesterol 0 mg

Sodium 211 mg

Total Carbs 52.8 g

Fiber 7.3 g

Sugar 25.5 g

Protein 9.1 g

Strawberry Oatmeal Smoothie

Ingredients

1½ cups frozen strawberries

1 medium banana, peeled and sliced

¼ cup old-fashioned oats

1 cup plain Greek yogurt

¾ cup unsweetened almond milk

How to Prepare

1. Add all the ingredients in a high-power blender and pulse until creamy.

2. Pour the smoothie into two glasses and serve immediately.

Preparation time: 10 minutes

Total time: 10 minutes

Servings: 2

Nutritional Values

Calories 227

Total Fat 4 g

Saturated Fat 1.5 g

Cholesterol 7 mg

Sodium 155 mg

Total Carbs 37.9 g

Fiber 5.1 g

Sugar 21.2 g

Protein 10 g

Blackberry Smoothie

Ingredients

1 cup frozen blackberries

1 large frozen banana, peeled and sliced

1/8 teaspoon vanilla extract

1½ cups unsweetened almond milk

How to Prepare

1.   Add all the ingredients in a high-power blender and pulse until creamy.

2.   Pour the smoothie into two glasses and serve immediately.

Preparation time: 10 minutes

Total time: 10 minutes

Servings: 2

Nutritional Values

Calories 114

Total 3.2 g

Saturated Fat 0.3 g

Cholesterol 0 mg

Sodium 136 mg

Total Carbs 21.9 g

Fiber 6.1 g

Sugar 10.8 g

Protein 2.4 g

Spirulina Blueberry Smoothie

Ingredients

1½ cups fresh blueberries

2 teaspoons blue spirulina powder

3–4 drops liquid stevia

1½ cups unsweetened almond milk

½ cup ice cubes

How to Prepare

1. Add all the ingredients in a high-power blender and pulse until creamy.

2. Pour the smoothie into two glasses and serve immediately.

Preparation time: 10 minutes

Total time: 10 minutes

Servings: 2

Nutritional Values

Calories 99

Total Fat 3.2 g

Saturated Fat 0.3 g

Cholesterol 0 mg

Sodium 160 mg

Total Carbs 17.8 g

Fiber 3.5 g

Sugar 10.9 g

Protein 2.9 g

Pear & Blueberry Smoothie

Ingredients

1 Asian pear; peeled, cored, and chopped

1 cup frozen blueberries

2 Medjool dates, pitted

3 tablespoons raw cashews

1 tablespoons hemp seeds

1¼ cups water

How to Prepare

1. Add all the ingredients in a high-power blender and pulse until creamy.

2. Pour the smoothie into two glasses and serve immediately.

Preparation time: 10 minutes

Total time: 10 minutes

Servings: 2

Nutritional Values

Calories 240

Total Fat 8.1 g

Saturated Fat 1.3 g

Cholesterol 0 mg

Sodium 8 mg

Total Carbs 42.1 g

Fiber 6 g

Sugar 28.8 g

Protein 4.8 g

Pineapple & Mango Smoothie

Ingredients

½ cup mango; peeled, pitted, and chopped

½ cup pineapple chunks

¼ teaspoon vanilla extract

½ cup plain Greek yogurt

¾ cup fresh orange juice

¼ cup ice cubes

How to Prepare

1. Add all the ingredients in a high-power blender and pulse until creamy.

2. Pour the smoothie into two glasses and serve immediately.

Preparation time: 10 minutes

Total time: 10 minutes

Servings: 2

Nutritional Values

Calories 132

Total Fat 1.2 g

Saturated Fat 0.7 g

Cholesterol 4 mg

Sodium 45 mg

Total Carbs 25.6 g

Fiber 1.4 g

Sugar 21.9 g

Protein 4.7 g

Orange Smoothie

Ingredients

1 cup unsweetened almond milk

2 medium oranges; peeled, seeded, and sectioned

2 tablespoons honey

¼ cup ice cubes

How to Prepare

1. Add all the ingredients in a high-power blender and pulse until creamy.

2. Pour the smoothie into two glasses and serve immediately.

Preparation time: 10 minutes

Total time: 10 minutes

Servings: 2

Nutritional Values

Calories 170

Total Fat 2 g

Saturated Fat 0.2 g

Cholesterol 0 mg

Sodium 91 mg

Total Carbs 39.9 g

Fiber 5 g

Sugar 34.5 g

Protein 2.3 g

Watermelon Smoothie

Ingredients

6½ cups seedless watermelon, chopped roughly

3 tablespoons fresh lime juice

How to Prepare

1. Add all the ingredients in a high-power blender and pulse until creamy.

2. Pour the smoothie into two glasses and serve immediately.

Preparation time: 10 minutes

Total time: 10 minutes

Servings: 2

Nutritional Values

Calories 150

Total Fat 0.7 g

Saturated Fat 0.3 g

Cholesterol 0 mg

Sodium 6 mg

Total Carbs 37.3 g

Fiber 1.9 g

Sugar 30.3 g

Protein 2.9 g

LOW-CARB SMOOTHIES RECIPES

Creamy Egg Smoothie

Ingredients

4 eggs

½ cup heavy whipping cream

4 tablespoons cream cheese, softened

1–2 tablespoons erythritol

½ teaspoon vanilla extract

½ cup ice cubes

How to Prepare

1. Add all the ingredients in a high-power blender and pulse until creamy.

2. Pour the smoothie into two glasses and serve immediately.

Preparation time: 10 minutes

Total time: 10 minutes

Servings: 2

Nutritional Values

Calories 302

Total Fat 26.8 g

Saturated Fat 14 g

Cholesterol 390 mg

Sodium 194 mg

Total Carbs 2.2g

Fiber 0 g

Sugar 0.9 g

Protein 13.2 g

Cheesy Egg Yolk Smoothie

Ingredients

4 large egg yolks

1 cup mascarpone cheese

1 tablespoon coconut oil

1 tablespoon erythritol

1 teaspoon vanilla extract

½ cup filtered water

¼ cup ice cubes

How to Prepare

1. Add all the ingredients in a high-power blender and pulse until creamy.

2. Pour the smoothie into two glasses and serve immediately.

Preparation time: 10 minutes

Total time: 10 minutes

Servings: 2

Nutritional Values

Calories 653

Total Fat 63.1g

Saturated Fat 9.1 g

Cholesterol 420 mg

Sodium 17 mg

Total Carbs 5.9 g

Fiber 0 g

Sugar 0.5 g

Protein 10.9 g

Mocha Smoothie

Ingredients

2 teaspoons instant espresso powder

2–3 tablespoons erythritol

2 teaspoons cacao powder

½ cup plain Greek yogurt

1 cup unsweetened almond milk

1 cup ice cubes

How to Prepare

1. Add all the ingredients in a high-power blender and pulse until creamy.

2. Pour the smoothie into two glasses and serve immediately.

Preparation time: 10 minutes

Total time: 10 minutes

Servings: 2

Nutritional Values

Calories 68

Total Fat 2.8 g

Saturated Fat 1 g

Cholesterol 4 mg

Sodium 133 mg

Total Carbs 6 g

Fiber 1 g

Sugar 4.3 g

Protein 4.3 g

Minty Chocolate Smoothie

Ingredients

½ ounce unsweetened dark chocolate, chopped

1 tablespoon fresh mint leaves

¼ teaspoon vanilla extract

2 tablespoons whipped cream

1¼ cups unsweetened almond milk

¼ cup ice cubes

How to Prepare

1. Add all the ingredients in a high-power blender and pulse until creamy.

2. Pour the smoothie into two glasses and serve immediately.

Preparation time: 10 minutes

Total time: 10 minutes

Servings: 2

Nutritional Values

Calories 119

Total Fat 10.6 g

Saturated Fat 5.5 g

Cholesterol 17 mg

Sodium 121 mg

Total Carbs 3.9 g

Fiber 1.8 g

Sugar 0.1 g

Protein 2 g

Chocolate Tahini Smoothie

Ingredients

½ cup heavy cream

1 tablespoon tahini

2 tablespoons cacao powder

8 drops liquid stevia

14 ounces chilled water

How to Prepare

1. Add all the ingredients in a high-power blender and pulse until creamy.

2. Pour the smoothie into two glasses and serve immediately.

Preparation time: 10 minutes

Total time: 10 minutes

Servings: 2

Nutritional Values

Calories 161

Total Fat 16.1 g

Saturated Fat 8.1 g

Cholesterol 41 mg

Sodium 20 mg

Total Carbs 4.9 g

Fiber 2.2 g

Sugar 0.1 g

Protein 2.9 g

Lettuce & Spinach Smoothie

Ingredients:

2 cups romaine lettuce, chopped

2 cups fresh baby spinach

¼ cup fresh mint leaves

2 tablespoons fresh lemon juice

8–10 drops liquid stevia

1½ cups filtered water

½ cup ice cubes

How to Prepare

1. Add all the ingredients in a high-power blender and pulse until creamy.

2. Pour the smoothie into two glasses and serve immediately.

Preparation time: 10 minutes

Total time: 10 minutes

Servings: 2

Nutritional Values

Calories 23

Total Fat 0.4 g

Saturated Fat 0.2 g

Cholesterol 0 mg

Sodium 33 mg

Total Carbs 4 g

Fiber 1.9 g

Sugar 1 g

Protein 1.6 g

Green Hemp Smoothie

Ingredients

1 tablespoon raw hemp seeds, shelled

2 cups fresh baby spinach

½ of avocado; peeled, pitted, and chopped

4–6 drops liquid stevia

¼ teaspoon ground cinnamon

2 cups chilled water

How to Prepare

1. Add all the ingredients in a high-power blender and pulse until creamy.

2. Pour the smoothie into two glasses and serve immediately.

Preparation time: 10 minutes

Total time: 10 minutes

Servings: 2

Nutritional Values

Calories 140

Total Fat 12.3 g

Saturated Fat 2.3 g

Cholesterol 0 mg

Sodium 27 mg

Total Carbs 6 g

Fiber 4.5 g

Sugar 0.4 g

Protein 3.5 g

Coconut Green Smoothie

Ingredients

2 cups fresh spinach

1 (1-inch) piece fresh ginger, peeled

¼ cup unsweetened ground coconut

¼ teaspoon salt

1½ cup unsweetened almond milk

1 cup ice

How to Prepare

1. Add all the ingredients in a high-power blender and pulse until creamy.

2. Pour the smoothie into two glasses and serve immediately.

Preparation time: 10 minutes

Total time: 10 minutes

Servings: 2

Nutritional Values

Calories 79

Total Fat 6.2 g

Saturated Fat 3.2 g

Cholesterol 0 mg

Sodium 454 mg

Total Carbs 5.3 g

Fiber 2.8 g

Sugar 0.8 g

Protein 2.5 g

Creamy Raspberry Smoothie

Ingredients

½ cup fresh raspberries

3 tablespoons heavy whipping cream

1/3 ounce cream cheese

1 cup unsweetened almond milk

½ cup ice, crushed

How to Prepare

1. Add all the ingredients in a high-power blender and pulse until creamy.

2. Pour the smoothie into two glasses and serve immediately.

Preparation time: 10 minutes

Total time: 10 minutes

Servings: 2

Nutritional Values

Calories 130

Total Fat 11.9 g

Saturated Fat 6.4 g

Cholesterol 36 mg

Sodium 113 mg

Total Carbs 5.4 g

Fiber 2.5 g

Sugar 1.4 g

Protein 1.7 g

PROTEIN SMOOTHIES RECIPES

Vanilla Smoothie

Ingredients

½ cup unsweetened vanilla whey protein powder

4 tablespoons almond butter

2 teaspoons vanilla extract

6–8 drops liquid stevia

2 cups unsweetened almond milk

¼ cup ice cubes

How to Prepare

1. Add all the ingredients in a high-power blender and pulse until creamy.

2. Pour the smoothie into two glasses and serve immediately.

Preparation time: 10 minutes

Total time: 10 minutes

Servings: 2

Nutritional Values

Calories 355

Total Fat 22.7 g

Saturated Fat 2 g

Cholesterol 24 mg

Sodium 231 mg

Total Carbs 10.4 g

Fiber 4.2 g

Sugar 3.2 g

Protein 29.8 g

Cottage Cheese Smoothie

Ingredients

½ cup cottage cheese

1 tablespoon natural peanut butter

2 scoops unsweetened whey protein powder

½ teaspoon vanilla extract

4–6 drops liquid stevia

1½ cups unsweetened almond milk

¼ cup ice cubes

How to Prepare

1.   Add all the ingredients in a high-power blender and pulse until creamy.

2.   Pour the smoothie into two glasses and serve immediately.

Preparation time: 10 minutes

Total time: 10 minutes

Servings: 2

Nutritional Values

Calories 240

Total Fat 8.9 g

Saturated Fat 2 g

Cholesterol 29 mg

Sodium 415 mg

Total Carbs 7 g

Fiber 1.3 g

Sugar 2 g

Protein 33.1 g

Chocolaty Egg Smoothie

Ingredients

3 large eggs

½ cup heavy whipping cream

¼ cup unsweetened whey protein powder

2 tablespoons cacao powder

2 tablespoons MCT oil

6–8 drops liquid stevia

½ teaspoon vanilla extract

½ cup filtered water

½ cup ice cubes

How to Prepare

1. Add all the ingredients in a high-power blender and pulse until creamy.

2. Pour the smoothie into two glasses and serve immediately.

Preparation time: 10 minutes

Total time: 10 minutes

Servings: 2

Nutritional Values

Calories 380

Total Fat 34.2 g

Saturated Fat 24 g

Cholesterol 332 mg

Sodium 141 mg

Total Carbs 5 g

Fiber 1.5 g

Sugar 1.4 g

Protein 22.1 g

Mocha Peppermint Smoothie

Ingredients

2 scoops unflavored collagen powder

4 tablespoons cacao powder

1 teaspoon vanilla extract

1 drop peppermint essential oil

6–8 drops liquid stevia

1 cup brewed coffee, frozen into ice cubes

1 cup unsweetened coconut milk

How to Prepare

1. Add all the ingredients in a high-power blender and pulse until creamy.

2. Pour the smoothie into two glasses and serve immediately.

Preparation time: 10 minutes

Total time: 10 minutes

Servings: 2

Nutritional Values

Calories 340

Total Fat 22 g

Saturated Fat 19.3 g

Cholesterol 0 mg

Sodium 83 mg

Total Carbs 11.3 g

Fiber 3 g

Sugar 2.3 g

Protein 30.6 g

Beetroot Powder Smoothie

Ingredients

2 scoops unsweetened whey protein powder

2 teaspoons beetroot powder

1 tablespoon MCT oil

1 teaspoon vanilla extract

¼ teaspoon ground cinnamon

3–4 drops liquid stevia

1¾ cup unsweetened almond milk

¼ cup ice cubes

How to Prepare

1. Add all the ingredients in a high-power blender and pulse until creamy.
2. Pour the smoothie into two glasses and serve immediately.

Preparation time: 10 minutes

Total time: 10 minutes

Servings: 2

Nutritional Values

Calories 208

Total Fat 11.3 g

Saturated Fat 7.6 g

Cholesterol 24 mg

Sodium 227 mg

Total Carbs 6.6 g

Fiber 1.5 g

Sugar 2 g

Protein 23.4 g

Cranberry Smoothie

Ingredients

1 cup fresh cranberries

1½ scoops unsweetened protein powder

1 teaspoon vanilla extract

3–4 drops liquid stevia

1¼ cups unsweetened almond milk

½ cup ice cubes

How to Prepare

1. Add all the ingredients in a high-power blender and pulse until creamy.

2. Pour the smoothie into two glasses and serve immediately.

Preparation time: 10 minutes

Total time: 10 minutes

Servings: 2

Nutritional Values

Calories 148

Total Fat 3 g

Saturated Fat 0.2 g

Cholesterol 0 mg

Sodium 311 mg

Total Carbs 6.5 g

Fiber 2.6 g

Sugar 2.3 g

Protein 19.6 g

Pumpkin Smoothie

Ingredients

1 cup canned pumpkin

1 cup unsweetened whey protein powder

¼–½ teaspoon stevia powder

½ teaspoon pumpkin pie spice

1 teaspoon vanilla extract

3 cups unsweetened almond milk

1 cup ice cubes, crushed

How to Prepare

1. Add all the ingredients in a high-power blender and pulse until creamy.

2. Pour the smoothie into four glasses and serve immediately.

Preparation time: 10 minutes

Total time: 10 minutes

Servings: 4

Nutritional Values

Calories 171

Total Fat 3.9 g

Saturated Fat 0.3 g

Cholesterol 0 mg

Sodium 402 mg

Total Carbs 6.7 g

Fiber 2.6 g

Sugar 2.2 g

Protein 26.8 g

Avocado Chia Seed Smoothie

Ingredients

½ of medium avocado; peeled, pitted, and chopped

1 scoop unflavored collagen powder

1 tablespoon chia seeds, soaked in 1 cup water for 15 minutes

1 cup heavy whipping cream

1 tablespoon almond butter

½ cup ice cubes

How to Prepare

1. Add all the ingredients in a high-power blender and pulse until creamy.

2. Pour the smoothie into two glasses and serve immediately.

Preparation time: 10 minutes

Total time: 10 minutes

Servings: 2

Nutritional Values

Calories 411

Total Fat 36.2 g

Saturated Fat 16 g

Cholesterol 82 mg

Sodium 41 mg

Total Carbs 8.3 g

Fiber 4.9 g

Sugar 0.6 g

Protein 18.2 g

Nutty Spinach Smoothie

Ingredients

2 cups fresh spinach

2 tablespoons almonds

2 tablespoons walnuts

2 scoops unsweetened whey protein

1 tablespoon psyllium seeds

1 tablespoon erythritol

1½ cups unsweetened almond milk

How to Prepare

1. Add all the ingredients in a high-power blender and pulse until creamy.

2. Pour the smoothie into two glasses and serve immediately.

Preparation time: 10 minutes

Total time: 10 minutes

Servings: 2

Nutritional Values

Calories 236

Total Fat 11.9 g

Saturated Fat 1.8 g

Cholesterol 69 mg

Sodium 217 mg

Total Carbs 10.8 g

Fiber 6.2 g

Sugar 3.6 g

Protein 28 g

Matcha Spinach & Avocado Smoothie

Ingredients

1 small avocado; peeled, pitted, and chopped

1¼ cups fresh spinach

½ cup unsweetened vanilla whey protein powder

1 tablespoon MCT oil

2 teaspoons vanilla extract

1 teaspoon matcha green tea powder

2 tablespoons golden monk fruit sweetener

½ cup heavy cream

½ cup filtered water

10 ice cubes

How to Prepare

1.   Add all the ingredients in a high-power blender and pulse until creamy.

2.   Pour the smoothie into two glasses and serve immediately.

Preparation time: 10 minutes

Total time: 10 minutes

Servings: 2

Nutritional Values

Calories 402

Total Fat 30.3 g

Saturated Fat 16.2 g

Cholesterol 41 mg

Sodium 294 mg

Total Carbs 6.9 g

Fiber 4.2 g

Sugar 0.9 g

Protein 27.6 g

WEIGHT LOSS SMOOTHIES RECIPES

Egg, Tomato & Carrot Smoothie

Ingredients

1 cup carrot, peeled and chopped

1 cup tomato, chopped roughly

1 boiled egg, peeled

Pinch of salt

1¼ cups chilled water

How to Prepare

1. Add all the ingredients in a high-power blender and pulse until creamy.

2. Pour the smoothie into two glasses and serve immediately.

Preparation time: 10 minutes

Total time: 10 minutes

Servings: 2

Nutritional Values

Calories 70

Total Fat 2.4 g

Saturated Fat 0.7 g

Cholesterol 82 mg

Sodium 151 mg

Total Carbs 9.1 g

Fiber 2.4 g

Sugar 5.2 g

Protein 4 g

Strawberry & Beet Smoothie

Ingredients

¾ cup raw red beets, chopped

1 cup frozen strawberries

2–3 drops liquid stevia

1½ cups unsweetened almond milk

½ cup ice cubes

How to Prepare

1. Add all the ingredients in a high-power blender and pulse until creamy.

2. Pour the smoothie into two glasses and serve immediately.

Preparation time: 10 minutes

Total time: 10 minutes

Servings: 2

Nutritional Values

Calories 81

Total Fat 3 g

Saturated Fat 0.3 g

Cholesterol 0 mg

Sodium 185 mg

Total Carbs 13.4 g

Fiber 3.5 g

Sugar 8.6 g

Protein 2.3 g

Cherry Smoothie

Ingredients

1 cup fresh cherries

Pinch of ground cinnamon

3–4 drops liquid stevia

1½ cups unsweetened almond milk

½ cup ice cubes

How to Prepare

1. Add all the ingredients in a high-power blender and pulse until creamy.

2. Pour the smoothie into two glasses and serve immediately.

Preparation time: 10 minutes

Total time: 10 minutes

Servings: 2

Nutritional Values

Calories 75

Total Fat 2.6 g

Saturated Fat 0.2 g

Cholesterol 0 mg

Sodium 135 mg

Total Carbs 12.6 g

Fiber 2.3 g

Sugar 9.5 g

Protein 1.8 g

Strawberry Smoothie

Ingredients

1 cup frozen strawberries

1 frozen banana, peeled and sliced

1 cup unsweetened almond milk

½ cup fresh orange juice

How to Prepare

1. Add all the ingredients in a high-power blender and pulse until creamy.

2. Pour the smoothie into two glasses and serve immediately.

Preparation time: 10 minutes

Total time: 10 minutes

Servings: 2

Nutritional Values

Calories 124

Total Fat 2.3 g

Saturated Fat 0.2 g

Cholesterol 0 mg

Sodium 92 mg

Total Carbs 26.5 g

Fiber 3.6 g

Sugar 16 g

Protein 2 g

Banana & Apple Smoothie

Ingredients

1 frozen bananas, peeled and sliced

1 green apple; peeled, cored, and chopped

1¼ cups unsweetened almond milk

½ cup ice cubes

How to Prepare

1.   Add all the ingredients in a high-power blender and pulse until creamy.

2.   Pour the smoothie into two glasses and serve immediately.

Preparation time: 10 minutes

Total time: 10 minutes

Servings: 2

Nutritional Values

Calories 113

Total Fat 2.6 g

Saturated Fat 0.3 g

Cholesterol 0 mg

Sodium 113 mg

Total Carbs 22.7 g

Fiber 3.2 g

Sugar 14.2 g

Protein 1.4 g

Apricot, Peach & Carrot Smoothie

Ingredients

4 apricots, pitted and chopped

2 peaches, pitted and chopped

1 medium carrot, peeled and chopped

1½ cups filtered water

¼ cup ice cubes

How to Prepare

1. Add all the ingredients in a high-power blender and pulse until creamy.

2. Pour the smoothie into two glasses and serve immediately.

Preparation time: 10 minutes

Total time: 10 minutes

Servings: 2

Nutritional Values

Calories 105

Total Fat 0.9 g

Saturated Fat 0 g

Cholesterol 0 mg

Sodium 22 mg

Total Carbs 24.7 g

Fiber 4.4 g

Sugar 21.8 g

Protein 2.6 g

Carrot, Tomato & Celery Smoothie

Ingredients

4 medium tomatoes

1 large carrot, peeled and chopped

1 celery stalk, chopped

Pinch of salt

¼ teaspoon ground black pepper

2 teaspoons fresh lemon juice

1 cup ice cubes

How to Prepare

1. Add all the ingredients in a high-power blender and pulse until creamy.

2. Pour the smoothie into two glasses and serve immediately.

Preparation time: 10 minutes

Total time: 10 minutes

Servings: 2

Nutritional Values

Calories 62

Total Fat 0.6 g

Saturated Fat 0.1 g

Cholesterol 0 mg

Sodium 122 mg

Total Carbs 13.6 g

Fiber 4.1 g

Sugar 8.5 g

Protein 2.6 g

Apple, Cucumber & Spinach Smoothie

Ingredients

2 large green apples; peeled, cored, and chopped

2 cups fresh baby spinach

1 small cucumber, peeled and chopped

1½ cups filtered water

¼ cup ice cubes

How to Prepare

1. Add all the ingredients in a high-power blender and pulse until creamy.

2. Pour the smoothie into two glasses and serve immediately.

Preparation time: 10 minutes

Total time: 10 minutes

Servings: 2

Nutritional Values

Calories 145

Total Fat 0.7 g

Saturated Fat 0.1 g

Cholesterol 0 mg

Sodium 29 mg

Total Carbs 37.4 g

Fiber 6.8 g

Sugar 25.8 g

Protein 2.4 g

Spinach, Strawberry & Orange Smoothie

Ingredients

1 cup frozen strawberries

2 cups fresh spinach

1 cup fresh orange juice

1 cup water

How to Prepare

1. Add all the ingredients in a high-power blender and pulse until creamy.

2. Pour the smoothie into two glasses and serve immediately.

Preparation time: 10 minutes

Total time: 10 minutes

Servings: 2

Nutritional Values

Calories 86

Total Fat 0.6 g

Saturated Fat 0.1 g

Cholesterol 0 mg

Sodium 25 mg

Total Carbs 19.5 g

Fiber 2.4 g

Sugar 14.1 g

Protein 2.2 g

Peach & Mango Smoothie

Ingredients

1 cup fresh peach, pitted and chopped

½ cup frozen mango; peeled, pitted, and cubed

1 teaspoon honey

½ cup fat-free plain yogurt

1 cup unsweetened almond milk

How to Prepare

1. Add all the ingredients in a high-power blender and pulse until creamy.

2. Pour the smoothie into two glasses and serve immediately.

Preparation time: 10 minutes

Total time: 10 minutes

Servings: 2

Nutritional Values

Calories 119

Total Fat 2.2 g

Saturated Fat 0.3 g

Cholesterol 1 mg

Sodium 138 mg

Total Carbs 21.8 g

Fiber 2.3 g

Sugar 20.2 g

Protein 5.1 g

ALKALINE SMOOTHIES RECIPES

Blackberry & Spinach Smoothie

Ingredients

¾ cup fresh blackberries

2 cups fresh spinach leaves

¼ cup fresh mint leaves

1 tablespoon sunflower seeds

1 tablespoon pumpkin seeds

1½ cups unsweetened almond milk

¼ cup ice cubes

How to Prepare

1. Add all the ingredients in a high-power blender and pulse until creamy.

2. Pour the smoothie into two glasses and serve immediately.

Preparation time: 10 minutes

Total time: 10 minutes

Servings: 2

Nutritional Values

Calories 97

Total Fat 5.8 g

Saturated Fat 0.7 g

Cholesterol 0 mg

Sodium 164 mg

Total Carbs 9.8 g

Fiber 5.3 g

Sugar 2.9 g

Protein 4.1 g

Strawberries Orange Smoothie

Ingredients

1 cup fresh strawberries, hulled and sliced

½ cup fresh raspberries

3–4 drops liquid stevia

1 cup fresh orange juice

¼ cup ice cubes

How to Prepare

1. Add all the ingredients in a high-power blender and pulse until creamy.

2. Pour the smoothie into two glasses and serve immediately.

Preparation time: 10 minutes

Total time: 10 minutes

Servings: 2

Nutritional Values

Calories 95

Total Fat 0.7 g

Saturated Fat 0.1 g

Cholesterol 0 mg

Sodium 2 mg

Total Carbs 22.1 g

Fiber 3.7 g

Sugar 15.3 g

Protein 1.7 g

Raspberry Smoothie

Ingredients

1 cup frozen raspberries

1 tablespoon coconut oil

1 scoop unflavored collagen powder

2–3 drops liquid stevia

1½ cups unsweetened almond milk

¼ cup ice cubes

How to Prepare

1. Add all the ingredients in a high-power blender and pulse until creamy.

2. Pour the smoothie into two glasses and serve immediately.

Preparation time: 10 minutes

Total time: 10 minutes

Servings: 2

Nutritional Values

Calories 174

Total Fat 9.8 g

Saturated Fat 6.1 g

Cholesterol 0 mg

Sodium 151 mg

Total Carbs 8.8 g

Fiber 4.8 g

Sugar 2.7 g

Protein 15.2 g

Banana & Pineapple Smoothie

Ingredients

1 large frozen banana

1 cup frozen pineapple chunks

¼ teaspoon vanilla extract

1½ cups unsweetened almond milk

How to Prepare

1. Add all the ingredients in a high-power blender and pulse until creamy.

2. Pour the smoothie into two glasses and serve immediately.

Preparation time: 10 minutes

Total time: 10 minutes

Servings: 2

Nutritional Values

Calories 125

Total Fat 2.9 g

Saturated Fat 0.3 g

Cholesterol 0 mg

Sodium 137 mg

Total Carbs 25.9 g

Fiber 3.4 g

Sugar 15.4 g

Protein 1.8 g

Papaya Smoothie

Ingredients

2 cups papaya, peeled and sliced

1 cup unsweetened almond milk

½ cup ice cubes

How to Prepare

1. Add all the ingredients in a high-power blender and pulse until creamy.

2. Pour the smoothie into two glasses and serve immediately.

Preparation time: 10 minutes

Total time: 10 minutes

Servings: 2

Nutritional Values

Calories 82

Total Fat 2.2 g

Saturated Fat 0.3 g

Cholesterol 0 mg

Sodium 102 mg

Total Carbs 16.7 g

Fiber 3 g

Sugar 11.3 g

Protein 1.2 g

Peach & Raspberry Smoothie

Ingredients

1 cup frozen peaches

½ cup frozen raspberries

2 tablespoons old fashioned oats

¼ teaspoon vanilla extract

¼ teaspoon ground cinnamon

1 cup oat milk

½ cup filtered water

How to Prepare

1. Add all the ingredients in a high-power blender and pulse until creamy.

2. Pour the smoothie into two glasses and serve immediately.

Preparation time: 10 minutes

Total time: 10 minutes

Servings: 2

Nutritional Values

Calories 180

Total Fat 1.9 g

Saturated Fat 0.1 g

Cholesterol 0 mg

Sodium 53 mg

Total Carbs 39 g

Fiber 5.6 g

Sugar 30.2 g

Protein 3.8 g

Apple Smoothie

Ingredients

1 medium red delicious apple, peeled and sliced

1 small ripe banana, peeled and sliced

¼ cup old-fashioned oats

1½ cups unsweetened almond milk

½ teaspoon ground cinnamon

1 cup ice cubes

How to Prepare

1. Add all the ingredients in a high-power blender and pulse until creamy.

2. Pour the smoothie into two glasses and serve immediately.

Preparation time: 10 minutes

Total time: 10 minutes

Servings: 2

Nutritional Values

Calories 179

Total Fat 3.7 g

Saturated Fat 0.4 g

Cholesterol 0 mg

Sodium 137 mg

Total Carbs 37.6 g

Fiber 6.3 g

Sugar 18.9 g

Protein 3 g

Apple, Carrot & Spinach Smoothie

Ingredients

2 tablespoons fresh lemon juice

1 green apple; peeled, cored, and chopped

1 carrot, peeled and chopped

2 cups fresh spinach, trimmed and chopped

1½ cups filtered water

¼ cup ice cubes

How to Prepare

1. Add all the ingredients in a high-power blender and pulse until creamy.

2. Pour the smoothie into two glasses and serve immediately.

Preparation time: 10 minutes

Total time: 10 minutes

Servings: 2

Nutritional Values

Calories 81

Total Fat 0.4 g

Saturated Fat 0.1 g

Cholesterol 0 mg

Sodium 49 mg

Total Carbs 19.8 g

Fiber 4.2 g

Sugar 13.6 g

Protein 1.5 g

Broccoli & Apple Smoothie

Ingredients

1 large green apple; peeled, cored, and chopped

½ cup broccoli florets, chopped

2 cups fresh kale leaves

1½ cups filtered water

¼ cup ice cubes

How to Prepare

1. Add all the ingredients in a high-power blender and pulse until creamy.

2. Pour the smoothie into two glasses and serve immediately.

Preparation time: 10 minutes

Total time: 10 minutes

Servings: 2

Nutritional Values

Calories 99

Total Fat 0.3 g

Saturated Fat 0 g

Cholesterol 0 mg

Sodium 38 mg

Total Carbs 23.9 g

Fiber 4.3 g

Sugar 12 g

Protein 2.9 g

Matcha Acai Smoothie

Ingredients

½ of medium avocado

1 pack unsweetened acai puree

2 tablespoons almond butter

2 tablespoons matcha green tea powder

4–5 drops liquid stevia

1½ cups unsweetened almond milk

How to Prepare

1. Add all the ingredients in a high-power blender and pulse until creamy.

2. Pour the smoothie into two glasses and serve immediately.

Preparation time: 10 minutes

Total time: 10 minutes

Servings: 2

Nutritional Values

Calories 305

Total Fat 27.6 g

Saturated Fat 3.5 g

Cholesterol 0 mg

Sodium 500 mg

Total Carbs 12.9 g

Fiber 7.5 g

Sugar 1.2 g

Protein 7.1 g

DIABETIC-FRIENDLY SMOOTHIES RECIPES

Kale & Avocado Smoothie

Ingredients

2 cups fresh baby kale

½ of avocado; peeled, pitted, and chopped

1 tablespoon raw hemp seeds, shelled

4–6 drops liquid stevia

½ teaspoon ground cinnamon

2 cups chilled water

How to Prepare

1. Add all the ingredients in a high-power blender and pulse until creamy.

2. Pour the smoothie into two glasses and serve immediately.

Preparation time: 10 minutes

Total time: 10 minutes

Servings: 2

Nutritional Values

Calories 163

Total 11.8 g

Saturated Fat 2.2 g

Cholesterol 0 mg

Sodium 32 mg

Total Carbs 11.1 g

Fiber 5 g

Sugar 0.6 g

Protein 5.3 g

Spinach & Avocado Smoothie

Ingredients

½ of large avocado; peeled, pitted, and chopped roughly

2 cups fresh spinach

2–3 drops liquid stevia

1½ cups unsweetened almond milk

How to Prepare

1. Add all the ingredients in a high-power blender and pulse until creamy.

2. Pour the smoothie into two glasses and serve immediately.

Preparation time: 10 minutes

Total time: 10 minutes

Servings: 2

Nutritional Values

Calories 153

Total Fat 13.8 g

Saturated Fat 2.6 g

Cholesterol 0 mg

Sodium 162 mg

Total Carbs 7.5 g

Fiber 5.2 g

Sugar 0.4 g

Protein 2.7 g

Kiwi & Avocado Smoothie

Ingredients

1 kiwi, peeled and chopped

1 small avocado; peeled, pitted, and chopped

1 cup cucumber, peeled and chopped

2 cups fresh baby kale

¼ cup fresh mint leaves

2 cups filtered water

¼ cup ice cubes

How to Prepare

1. Add all the ingredients in a high-power blender and pulse until creamy.

2. Pour the smoothie into two glasses and serve immediately.

Preparation time: 10 minutes

Total time: 10 minutes

Servings: 2

Nutritional Values

Calories 185

Total Fat 11.4 g

Saturated Fat 2.4 g

Cholesterol 0 mg

Sodium 38 mg

Total Carbs 20.3 g

Fiber 7 g

Sugar 4.6 g

Protein 4.2 g

Matcha Chia Seed Smoothie

Ingredients

2 tablespoons chia seeds

2 teaspoons matcha green tea powder

½ teaspoon fresh lime juice

6–8 drops liquid stevia

¼ cup coconut yogurt

1¼ cups unsweetened coconut milk

¼ cup ice cubes

How to Prepare

1. Add all the ingredients in a high-power blender and pulse until creamy.

2. Pour the smoothie into two glasses and serve immediately.

Preparation time: 10 minutes

Total time: 10 minutes

Servings: 2

Nutritional Values

Calories 276

Total Fat 24.5 g

Saturated Fat 20.2 g

Cholesterol 1 mg

Sodium 54 mg

Total Carbs 8.2 g

Fiber 2.5 g

Sugar 4.8 g

Protein 4.9 g

Zucchini & Spinach Smoothie

Ingredients

1 small zucchini, peeled and sliced

¾ cup fresh spinach, chopped

1 teaspoon ground cinnamon

4–6 drops liquid stevia

1½ cups unsweetened almond milk

½ cup ice cubes

How to Prepare

1. Add all the ingredients in a high-power blender and pulse until creamy.

2. Pour the smoothie into two glasses and serve immediately.

Preparation time: 10 minutes

Total time: 10 minutes

Servings: 2

Nutritional Values

Calories 45

Total Fat 2.8 g

Saturated Fat 0.3 g

Cholesterol 0 mg

Sodium 150 mg

Total Carbs 4.8 g

Fiber 2.3 g

Sugar 1.1 g

Protein 1.8 g

Greens & Cucumber Smoothie

Ingredients

1 large cucumber, peeled and chopped

2 cups fresh baby greens

¼ cup fresh mint leaves

2 tablespoons fresh lime juice

2 cups chilled unsweetened almond milk

How to Prepare

1. Add all the ingredients in a high-power blender and pulse until creamy.

2. Pour the smoothie into two glasses and serve immediately.

Preparation time: 10 minutes

Total time: 10 minutes

Servings: 2

Nutritional Values

Calories 72

Total Fat 3.8 g

Saturated Fat 0.4 g

Cholesterol 0 mg

Sodium 190 mg

Total Carbs 9.2 g

Fiber 2.9 g

Sugar 2.9 g

Protein 2.7 g

Avocado & Mint Smoothie

Ingredients

1 avocado; peeled, pitted, and chopped

12–14 fresh large mint leaves

2 tablespoons fresh lime juice

½ teaspoon vanilla extract

1½ cups unsweetened almond milk

¼ cup ice, crushed

How to Prepare

1. Add all the ingredients in a high-power blender and pulse until creamy.

2. Pour the smoothie into two glasses and serve immediately.

Preparation time: 10 minutes

Total time: 10 minutes

Servings: 2

Nutritional Values

Calories 214

Total Fat 18.5 g

Saturated Fat 2.6 g

Cholesterol 0 mg

Sodium 45 mg

Total Carbs 11.7 g

Fiber 8.9 g

Sugar 0.4 g

Protein 3.3 g

Green Veggies Smoothie

Ingredients

1 cup fresh spinach

¼ cup broccoli florets, chopped

¼ cup green cabbage, chopped

½ of small green bell pepper, seeded and chopped

8–10 drops liquid stevia

2 cups chilled water

How to Prepare

1. Add all the ingredients in a high-power blender and pulse until creamy.

2. Pour the smoothie into two glasses and serve immediately.

Preparation time: 10 minutes

Total time: 10 minutes

Servings: 2

Nutritional Values

Calories 19

Total Fat 0.2 g

Saturated Fat 0 g

Cholesterol 0 mg

Sodium 18 mg

Total Carbs 4.1 g

Fiber 1.3 g

Sugar 2 g

Protein 1.2 g

Strawberry & Spinach Smoothie

Ingredients

2 cups fresh spinach

¾ cup frozen strawberries, sliced

4–6 drops liquid stevia

1½ cups unsweetened almond milk

How to Prepare

1. Add all the ingredients in a high-power blender and pulse until creamy.

2. Pour the smoothie into two glasses and serve immediately.

Preparation time: 10 minutes

Total time: 10 minutes

Servings: 2

Nutritional Values

Calories 54

Total Fat 2.9 g

Saturated Fat 0.3 g

Cholesterol 0 mg

Sodium 159 mg

Total Carbs 6.7 g

Fiber 2.5 g

Sugar 2.8 g

Protein 2 g

Kale & Celery Smoothie

Ingredients

2 cups fresh kale

1 celery stalk

½ of avocado; peeled, pitted, and chopped

1 teaspoon fresh ginger, peeled and chopped

1½ cups unsweetened almond milk

¼ cup ice cubes

How to Prepare

1. Add all the ingredients in a high-power blender and pulse until creamy.

2. Pour the smoothie into two glasses and serve immediately.

Preparation time: 10 minutes

Total time: 10 minutes

Servings: 2

Nutritional Values

Calories 170

Total Fat 12.5 g

Saturated Fat 2.3 g

Cholesterol 0 mg

Sodium 174 mg

Total Carbs 13.7 g

Fiber 5.4 g

Sugar 0.4 g

Protein 3.8 g

GREEN SMOOTHIES RECIPES

Avocado Smoothie

Ingredients

1 large avocado, pitted and sliced

1 tablespoon fresh lime juice

1 cup unsweetened almond milk

½ cup coconut water

¼ cup ice cubes

How to Prepare

1. Add all the ingredients in a high-power blender and pulse until creamy.

2. Pour the smoothie into two glasses and serve immediately.

Preparation time: 10 minutes

Total time: 10 minutes

Servings: 2

Nutritional Values

Calories 181

Total Fat 16.1 g

Saturated Fat 3.3 g

Cholesterol 0 mg

Sodium 158 mg

Total Carbs 9.5 g

Fiber 6.1 g

Sugar 1.9 g

Protein 2.3 g

Cucumber & Parsley Smoothie

Ingredients

2 cups cucumber, peeled and chopped

2 cups fresh parsley

1 (1-inch) piece fresh ginger root, peeled and chopped

2 tablespoons fresh lemon juice

4–6 drops liquid stevia

2 cups chilled water

How to Prepare

1. Add all the ingredients in a high-power blender and pulse until creamy.

2. Pour the smoothie into two glasses and serve immediately.

Preparation time: 10 minutes

Total time: 10 minutes

Servings: 2

Nutritional Values

Calories 44

Total Fat 0.8 g

Saturated Fat 0.3 g

Cholesterol 0 mg

Sodium 39 mg

Total Carbs 8.5 g

Fiber 2.7 g

Sugar 2.6 g

Protein 2.7 g

Grapes Smoothie

Ingredients

2 cups seedless green grapes

1 tablespoon honey

½ cup fresh apple juice

1 cup unsweetened almond milk

¼ cup ice cubes

How to Prepare

1. Add all the ingredients in a high-power blender and pulse until creamy.

2. Pour the smoothie into two glasses and serve immediately.

Preparation time: 10 minutes

Total time: 10 minutes

Servings: 2

Nutritional Values

Calories 196

Total Fat 1.8 g

Saturated Fat 0.2 g

Cholesterol 0 mg

Sodium 96 mg

Total Carbs 46.7 g

Fiber 1.8 g

Sugar 40.2 g

Protein 0.6 g

Kale & Cucumber Smoothie

Ingredients

2 teaspoons green spirulina powder

1½ cups fresh kale

1 cup cucumber, peeled and chopped

1 tablespoon chia seeds

1½ cups unsweetened almond milk

¼ cup ice cubes

How to Prepare

1. Add all the ingredients in a high-power blender and pulse until creamy.

2. Pour the smoothie into two glasses and serve immediately.

Preparation time: 10 minutes

Total time: 10 minutes

Servings: 2

Nutritional Values

Calories 84

Total Fat 4.1 g

Saturated Fat 0.4 g

Cholesterol 0 mg

Sodium 182 mg

Total Carbs 10.7 g

Fiber 3.1 g

Sugar 0.9 g

Protein 4.7 g

Strawberry, Cucumber & Greens Smoothie

Ingredients

1 cup fresh strawberries, hulled and sliced

1 cup fresh kale, trimmed and chopped

1 cup fresh spinach, chopped

½ cucumber, peeled and chopped

1½ cups unsweetened almond milk

¼ cup ice cubes

How to Prepare

1. Add all the ingredients in a high-power blender and pulse until creamy.

2. Pour the smoothie into two glasses and serve immediately.

Preparation time: 10 minutes

Total time: 10 minutes

Servings: 2

Nutritional Values

Calories 84

Total Fat 3 g

Saturated Fat 0.3 g

Cholesterol 0 mg

Sodium 164 mg

Total Carbs 13.8 g

Fiber 3.4 g

Sugar 4.9 g

Protein 3.2 g

Kiwi & Banana Smoothie

Ingredients

1 large frozen banana, peeled and sliced

3 kiwis, peeled and sliced

1 cup fat-free plain yogurt

½ cup ice cubes

How to Prepare

1. Add all the ingredients in a high-power blender and pulse until creamy.

2. Pour the smoothie into two glasses and serve immediately.

Preparation time: 10 minutes

Total time: 10 minutes

Servings: 2

Nutritional Values

Calories 185

Total Fat 0.9 g

Saturated Fat 0.1 g

Cholesterol 2 mg

Sodium 90 mg

Total Carbs 40.7 g

Fiber 5.2 g

Sugar 18.6 g

Protein 7 g

Green Sunflower Butter Smoothie

Ingredients

1 avocado; peeled, pitted, and chopped

2 cups fresh spinach

1 scoop unflavored collagen protein powder

1 tablespoon sunflower seed butter

1 teaspoon vanilla extract

½ tablespoon MCT oil

8–10 drops liquid stevia

1 cup unsweetened almond milk

1 cup ice cubes

How to Prepare

1.   Add all the ingredients in a high-power blender and pulse until creamy.

2.   Pour the smoothie into two glasses and serve immediately.

Preparation time: 10 minutes

Total time: 10 minutes

Servings: 2

Nutritional Values

Calories 282

Total Fat 25.8 g

Saturated Fat 7.6 g

Cholesterol 0 mg

Sodium 126 mg

Total Carbs 11.9 g

Fiber 6.9 g

Sugar 0.8 g

Protein 5.6 g

Cucumber & Mint Smoothie

Ingredients

1 large cucumber, peeled and chopped

1 cup fresh kale

¼ cup fresh mint leaves

2 tablespoons fresh lemon juice

1½ cups unsweetened almond milk

¼ cup ice, crushed

How to Prepare

1. Add all the ingredients in a high-power blender and pulse until creamy.

2. Pour the smoothie into two glasses and serve immediately.

Preparation time: 10 minutes

Total time: 10 minutes

Servings: 2

Nutritional Values

Calories 78

Total Fat 3 g

Saturated Fat 0.4 g

Cholesterol 0 mg

Sodium 159 mg

Total Carbs 11.7 g

Fiber 2.8 g

Sugar 2.8 g

Protein 3.2 g

Creamy Greens Smoothie

Ingredients

1 cup fresh baby spinach

1 cup fresh baby kale

1 tablespoon almond butter

1 tablespoon chia seeds

1/8 teaspoon ground cinnamon

Pinch of ground cloves

½ cup heavy cream

1 cup unsweetened almond milk

½ cup ice cubes

How to Prepare

1. Add all the ingredients in a high-power blender and pulse until creamy.

2. Pour the smoothie into two glasses and serve immediately.

Preparation time: 10 minutes

Total time: 10 minutes

Servings: 2

Nutritional Values

Calories 208

Total Fat 18.7 g

Saturated Fat 7.5 g

Cholesterol 41 mg

Sodium 129 mg

Total Carbs 9.1 g

Fiber 3.5 g

Sugar 0.4 g

Protein 5 g

Cucumber & Lettuce Smoothie

Ingredients

1 cucumber, peeled and chopped

1 cup lettuce leaves

½ cup fresh mint leaves

1 tablespoon fresh ginger, grated

2 cups coconut water

1 tablespoon fresh lime juice

¼ cup ice cubes

How to Prepare

1. Add all the ingredients in a high-power blender and pulse until creamy.

2. Pour the smoothie into two glasses and serve immediately.

Preparation time: 10 minutes

Total time: 10 minutes

Servings: 2

Nutritional Values

Calories 92

Total Fat 1 g

Saturated Fat 0.6 g

Cholesterol 0 mg

Sodium 265 mg

Total Carbs 19.1 g

Fiber 5.5 g

Sugar 9.1 g

Protein 3.8 g

DETOX SMOOTHIES RECIPES

Minty Green Smoothie

Ingredients

½ of avocado; peeled, pitted, and chopped

1 cup fresh kale leaves

½ of small cucumber, peeled and chopped

¼ cup fresh mint leaves

1 tablespoon almond butter

1 tablespoon fresh lemon juice

1¼ cups unsweetened almond milk

½ cup ice cubes

How to Prepare

1. Add all the ingredients in a high-power blender and pulse until creamy.

2. Pour the smoothie into two glasses and serve immediately.

Preparation time: 10 minutes

Total time: 10 minutes

Servings: 2

Nutritional Values

Calories 195

Total Fat 15.2 g

Saturated Fat 2.4 g

Cholesterol 0 mg

Sodium 137 mg

Total Carbs 13.8 g

Fiber 6 g

Sugar 2 g

Protein 5.1 g

Spiced Smoothie

Ingredients

2 tablespoons chia seeds

1 tablespoon ground turmeric

1 teaspoon ground cinnamon

1 teaspoon ground ginger

¼ teaspoon ground cardamom

Pinch of ground black pepper

2 tablespoons MCT oil

2 teaspoons stevia powder

1¾ cups unsweetened almond milk

¼ cup ice cubes

How to Prepare

1. Add all the ingredients in a high-power blender and pulse until creamy.
2. Pour the smoothie into two glasses and serve immediately.

Preparation time: 10 minutes

Total time: 10 minutes

Servings: 2

Nutritional Values

Calories 183

Total Fat 20 g

Saturated Fat 14.6 g

Cholesterol 0 mg

Sodium 159 mg

Total Carbs 8.7 g

Fiber 4.9 g

Sugar 0.2 g

Protein 2.8 g

Pineapple & Turmeric Smoothie

Ingredients

1½ cups pineapple, chopped

1 (1-inch) piece fresh ginger, peeled and chopped

1 teaspoon ground turmeric

1 teaspoon natural immune support

1 teaspoon chia seeds

1 cup cold green tea

½ cup ice, crushed

How to Prepare

1. Add all the ingredients in a high-power blender and pulse until creamy.

2. Pour the smoothie into two glasses and serve immediately.

Preparation time: 10 minutes

Total time: 10 minutes

Servings: 2

Nutritional Values

Calories 104

Total Fat 1.1 g

Saturated Fat 0.1 g

Cholesterol 0 mg

Sodium 12 mg

Total Carbs 24.9 g

Fiber 2.9 g

Sugar 18.8 g

Protein 1.3 g

Watermelon & Strawberry Smoothie

Ingredients

1½ cups fresh watermelon, seeded and cubed

1 cup frozen strawberries

½ of frozen banana, peeled and sliced

1 tablespoon hemp seeds

2 tablespoons fresh lime juice

1 cup unsweetened almond milk

How to Prepare

1. Add all the ingredients in a high-power blender and pulse until creamy.

2. Pour the smoothie into two glasses and serve immediately.

Preparation time: 10 minutes

Total time: 10 minutes

Servings: 2

Nutritional Values

Calories 126

Total Fat 3.9 g

Saturated Fat 0.4 g

Cholesterol 0 mg

Sodium 93 mg

Total Carbs 22.2 g

Fiber 3 g

Sugar 14.1 g

Protein 3.2 g

Grapefruit & Pineapple Smoothie

Ingredients

3 grapefruit; peeled, seeded, and chopped

½ cup frozen pineapple chunks

1½ cups unsweetened almond milk

¼ cup ice cubes

How to Prepare

1. Add all the ingredients in a high-power blender and pulse until creamy.

2. Pour the smoothie into two glasses and serve immediately.

Preparation time: 10 minutes

Total time: 10 minutes

Servings: 2

Nutritional Values

Calories 112

Total Fat 2.9 g

Saturated Fat 0.3 g

Cholesterol 0 mg

Sodium 136 mg

Total Carbs 22.4 g

Fiber 3.4 g

Sugar 17.5 g

Protein 2.2 g

Berries Yogurt Smoothie

Ingredients

1½ cups frozen mixed berries

½ teaspoon vanilla extract

1 cup plain yogurt

1 cup fresh orange juice

¼ cup ice cubes

How to Prepare

1. Add all the ingredients in a high-power blender and pulse until creamy.

2. Pour the smoothie into two glasses and serve immediately.

Preparation time: 10 minutes

Total time: 10 minutes

Servings: 2

Nutritional Values

Calories 206

Total Fat 2.1 g

Saturated Fat 1.3 g

Cholesterol 7 mg

Sodium 87 mg

Total Carbs 34.4 g

Fiber 4 g

Sugar 26.7 g

Protein 8.6 g

Cherry & Blueberry Smoothie

Ingredients

1¼ cups frozen blueberries

1 cup frozen unsweetened cherries

1 small banana, peeled and slice

6 ounces fat-free plain yogurt

1 cup unsweetened almond milk

How to Prepare

1. Add all the ingredients in a high-power blender and pulse until creamy.

2. Pour the smoothie into two glasses and serve immediately.

Preparation time: 10 minutes

Total time: 10 minutes

Servings: 2

Nutritional Values

Calories 203

Total Fat 2.3 g

Saturated Fat 0.2 g

Cholesterol 2 mg

Sodium 156 mg

Total Carbs 43 g

Fiber 5.5 g

Sugar 24.7 g

Protein 6.5 g

Pineapple & Cucumber Smoothie

Ingredients

1 cup pineapple, chopped

1 cucumber, peeled and chopped

4 Medjool dates, pitted

2 tablespoons fresh lemon juice

1½ cups filtered water

How to Prepare

1.   Add all the ingredients in a high-power blender and pulse until creamy.

2.   Pour the smoothie into two glasses and serve immediately.

Preparation time: 10 minutes

Total time: 10 minutes

Servings: 2

Nutritional Values

Calories 193

Total Fat 0.4 g

Saturated Fat 0.2 g

Cholesterol 0 mg

Sodium 7 mg

Total Carbs 49.6 g

Fiber 5.1 g

Sugar 39.2 g

Protein 3.1 g

Carrot & Pineapple Smoothie

Ingredients

2 cups carrot, peeled and chopped

2 cups pineapple chunks

1 tablespoon fresh ginger, grated

1½ tablespoons fresh lemon juice

1 cup ice cubes

How to Prepare

1. Add all the ingredients in a high-power blender and pulse until creamy.

2. Pour the smoothie into two glasses and serve immediately.

Preparation time: 10 minutes

Total time: 10 minutes

Servings: 2

Nutritional Values

Calories 139

Total Fat 0.5 g

Saturated Fat 0.2 g

Cholesterol 0 mg

Sodium 81 mg

Total Carbs 34.6 g

Fiber 5.4 g

Sugar 22 g

Protein 2.1 g

Cranberry & Grapefruit Smoothie

Ingredients

½ cup fresh cranberries

2 grapefruit; peeled, seeded, and sectioned

1 frozen banana, peeled and sliced

1 tablespoon agave nectar

¾ cup fresh orange juice

½ cup unsweetened almond milk

¼ cup ice cubes

How to Prepare

1. Add all the ingredients in a high-power blender and pulse until creamy.

2. Pour the smoothie into two glasses and serve immediately.

Preparation time: 10 minutes

Total time: 10 minutes

Servings: 2

Nutritional Values

Calories 190

Total Fat 1.4 g

Saturated Fat 0.2 g

Cholesterol 0 mg

Sodium 46 mg

Total Carbs 44.5 g

Fiber 4.9 g

Sugar 32.5 g

Protein 2.3 g

HIGH-ENERGY SMOOTHIES RECIPES

Date & Almond Smoothie

Ingredients

1 cup Medjool dates, pitted and chopped

½ cup almonds, chopped

1½ cups unsweetened almond milk

¼ cup ice cubes

How to Prepare

1. Add all the ingredients in a high-power blender and pulse until creamy.

2. Pour the smoothie into two glasses and serve immediately.

Preparation time: 10 minutes

Total time: 10 minutes

Servings: 2

Nutritional Values

Calories 418

Total Fat 14.9 g

Saturated Fat 1.2 g

Cholesterol 0 mg

Sodium 137 mg

Total Carbs 73.4 g

Fiber 10.8 g

Sugar 57.4 g

Protein 8 g

Chocolaty Peanut Butter Smoothie

Ingredients

¼ cup creamy peanut butter

2 tablespoons cacao powder

8–10 drops liquid stevia

1 cup heavy cream

1 cup unsweetened almond milk

¼ cup ice cubes

How to Prepare

1. Add all the ingredients in a high-power blender and pulse until creamy.

2. Pour the smoothie into two glasses and serve immediately.

Preparation time: 10 minutes

Total time: 10 minutes

Servings: 2

Nutritional Values

Calories 429

Total Fat 41.2 g

Saturated Fat 18 g

Cholesterol 82 mg

Sodium 261 mg

Total Carbs 11.5 g

Fiber 3.9 g

Sugar 3.1 g

Protein 10.8 g

Banana Peanut Butter Smoothie

Ingredients

2 cups frozen bananas, peeled and sliced

2 tablespoons all-natural peanut butter

½ tablespoon ground flax seeds

1 teaspoon vanilla extract

½ cup plain Greek yogurt

1 cup unsweetened almond milk

How to Prepare

1. Add all the ingredients in a high-power blender and pulse until creamy.

2. Pour the smoothie into two glasses and serve immediately.

Preparation time: 10 minutes

Total time: 10 minutes

Servings: 2

Nutritional Values

Calories 312

Total Fat 11.6 g

Saturated Fat 2.5 g

Cholesterol 4 mg

Sodium 138 mg

Total Carbs 43.3 g

Fiber 5.9 g

Sugar 24 g

Protein 11 g

Raspberry Peanut Butter Smoothie

Ingredients

1 banana, peeled and sliced

2 cups fresh raspberries

2 tablespoons peanut butter

1 tablespoon honey

1½ cups unsweetened almond milk

¼ cup ice cubes

How to Prepare

1.   Add all the ingredients in a high-power blender and pulse until creamy.

2.   Pour the smoothie into two glasses and serve immediately.

Preparation time: 10 minutes

Total time: 10 minutes

Servings: 2

Nutritional Values

Calories 278

Total Fat 11.6 g

Saturated Fat 1.8 g

Cholesterol 0 mg

Sodium 140 mg

Total Carbs 41.3 g

Fiber 11.3 g

Sugar 22.3 g

Protein 7.9 g

Creamy Blackberry Smoothie

Ingredients

1 cup fresh blackberries

½ cup heavy whipping cream

½ cup cream cheese, softened

½ tablespoon coconut oil

3–5 drops liquid stevia

1 cup chilled water

How to Prepare

1. Add all the ingredients in a high-power blender and pulse until creamy.

2. Pour the smoothie into two glasses and serve immediately.

Preparation time: 10 minutes

Total time: 10 minutes

Servings: 2

Nutritional Values

Calories 366

Total Fat 35.1 g

Saturated Fat 22.6 g

Cholesterol 105 mg

Sodium 184 mg

Total Carbs 9.3 g

Fiber 3.8 g

Sugar 3.7g

Protein 6 g

Berries Cream Smoothie

Ingredients

1 cup mixed fresh berries

1 tablespoon MCT oil

½ teaspoon vanilla extract

3–5 drops liquid stevia

¾ cup heavy whipping cream

1 cup unsweetened almond milk

¼ cup ice cubes

How to Prepare

1. Add all the ingredients in a high-power blender and pulse until creamy.

2. Pour the smoothie into two glasses and serve immediately.

Preparation time: 10 minutes

Total time: 10 minutes

Servings: 2

Nutritional Values

Calories 268

Total Fat 25.7 g

Saturated Fat 17.5 g

Cholesterol 62 mg

Sodium 108 mg

Total Carbs 10.9 g

Fiber 3 g

Sugar 2.2 g

Protein 1.9 g

Kiwi & Melon Smoothie

Ingredients

2 kiwi fruit, peeled and chopped

1 cup honeydew melon, peeled and chopped

½ teaspoon fresh ginger, chopped

1½ scoops unsweetened protein powder

½ tablespoon fresh lime juice

1¾ cups fresh grape juice

¼ cup ice cubes

How to Prepare

1. Add all the ingredients in a high-power blender and pulse until creamy.

2. Pour the smoothie into two glasses and serve immediately.

Preparation time: 10 minutes

Total time: 10 minutes

Servings: 2

Nutritional Values

Calories 314

Total Fat 1.8 g

Saturated Fat 0.1 g

Cholesterol 0 mg

Sodium 217 mg

Total Carbs 53.8 g

Fiber 3.4 g

Sugar 48.5 g

Protein 22.7 g

Sweet Potato Smoothie

Ingredients

1 medium frozen banana, peeled and sliced

1 cup sweet potato puree

1 teaspoon fresh ginger, chopped

½ tablespoon flax seeds meal

1 tablespoon almond butter

¼ teaspoon ground turmeric

¼ teaspoon ground cinnamon

1 cup unsweetened almond milk

¼ cup fresh orange juice

¼ cup ice cubes

How to Prepare

1. Add all the ingredients in a high-power blender and pulse until creamy.

2. Pour the smoothie into two glasses and serve immediately.

Preparation time: 10 minutes

Total time: 10 minutes

Servings: 2

Nutritional Values

Calories 242

Total Fat 7.5 g

Saturated Fat 0.7 g

Cholesterol 0 mg

Sodium 128 mg

Total Carbs 41.7 g

Fiber 7.1 g

Sugar 16.7 g

Protein 5.7 g

Pumpkin & Banana Smoothie

Ingredients

¾ cup pumpkin puree

2 medium frozen bananas, peeled and sliced

½ teaspoon pumpkin pie spice

1 scoop unsweetened whey protein powder

4–6 drops liquid stevia

½ cup plain Greek yogurt

1 cup unsweetened almond milk

How to Prepare

1. Add all the ingredients in a high-power blender and pulse until creamy.

2. Pour the smoothie into two glasses and serve immediately.

Preparation time: 10 minutes

Total time: 10 minutes

Servings: 2

Nutritional Values

Calories 259

Total Fat 3.7 g

Saturated Fat 1.1 g

Cholesterol 4 mg

Sodium 271 mg

Total Carbs 40 g

Fiber 6.3 g

Sugar 21.8 g

Protein 19 g

Matcha Spinach & Pineapple Smoothie

Ingredients

½ cup frozen pineapple

1 cup fresh baby spinach

½ of avocado; peeled, pitted, and chopped

2 tablespoons honey

1 tablespoon coconut oil

1 teaspoon matcha green tea powder

½ cup fresh orange juice

1 cup unsweetened almond milk

How to Prepare

1. Add all the ingredients in a high-power blender and pulse until creamy.

2. Pour the smoothie into two glasses and serve immediately.

Preparation time: 10 minutes

Total time: 10 minutes

Servings: 2

Nutritional Values

Calories 297

Total Fat 18.6 g

Saturated Fat 8.1 g

Cholesterol 0 mg

Sodium 107 mg

Total Carbs 35 g

Fiber 5 g

Sugar 26.8 g

Protein 2.6 g

BRAIN-HEALTHY SMOOTHIES RECIPES

Chocolate Smoothie

Ingredients

2 cups fresh spinach

½ cup fresh blueberries

2 Medjool dates, pitted

1–2 tablespoons raw cacao nibs

1 tablespoon ground chia seeds

1 cup unsweetened cashew milk

¼ cup ice cubes

How to Prepare

1. Add all the ingredients in a high-power blender and pulse until creamy.
2. Pour the smoothie into two glasses and serve immediately.

Preparation time: 10 minutes

Total time: 10 minutes

Servings: 2

Nutritional Values

Calories 148

Total Fat 4.1 g

Saturated Fat 1.1 g

Cholesterol 0 mg

Sodium 106 mg

Total Carbs 27.4 g

Fiber 6.8 g

Sugar 17.9 g

Protein 3.3 g

Coffee Chia Smoothie

Ingredients

1 tablespoon chia seeds

1 tablespoon MCT oil

½ teaspoon ground cinnamon

½ cup heavy whipping cream

12 ounces cold brewed coffee

½ cup unsweetened almond milk

How to Prepare

1. Add all the ingredients in a high-power blender and pulse until creamy.

2. Pour the smoothie into two glasses and serve immediately.

Preparation time: 10 minutes

Total time: 10 minutes

Servings: 2

Nutritional Values

Calories 181

Total Fat 20.3 g

Saturated Fat 14.1 g

Cholesterol 41 mg

Sodium 60 mg

Total Carbs 3.3 g

Fiber 1.8 g

Sugar 0 g

Protein 1.8 g

Berries, Kale & Avocado Smoothie

Ingredients

1 cup frozen blueberries

1 cup fresh kale leaves

½ of avocado

3 Medjool dates, pitted

½ teaspoon green spirulina powder

2 cups soy milk

How to Prepare

1. Add all the ingredients in a high-power blender and pulse until creamy.

2. Pour the smoothie into two glasses and serve immediately.

Preparation time: 10 minutes

Total time: 10 minutes

Servings: 2

Nutritional Values

Calories 389

Total Fat 14.3 g

Saturated Fat 2.6 g

Cholesterol 0 mg

Sodium 149 mg

Total Carbs 58.6 g

Fiber 9.5 g

Sugar 38.5 g

Protein 12 g

Berries & Pomegranate Smoothie

Ingredients

2 cups mixed fresh berries

2 tablespoons chia seeds

1¼ cups fresh pomegranate juice

¾ cup filtered water

How to Prepare

1. Add all the ingredients in a high-power blender and pulse until creamy.

2. Pour the smoothie into two glasses and serve immediately.

Preparation time: 10 minutes

Total time: 10 minutes

Servings: 2

Nutritional Values

Calories 209

Total Fat 3 g

Saturated Fat 0.2 g

Cholesterol 0 mg

Sodium 13 mg

Total Carbs 45 g

Fiber 7.5 g

Sugar 31.3 g

Protein 2.5 g

Blueberry & Avocado Smoothie

Ingredients

2 cups fresh blueberries

1 large banana, peeled and sliced

1 small avocado; peeled, pitted, and chopped

1 tablespoon chia seeds

1 cup fresh cranberry juice

¼ cup ice cubes

How to Prepare

1. Add all the ingredients in a high-power blender and pulse until creamy.

2. Pour the smoothie into two glasses and serve immediately.

Preparation time: 10 minutes

Total time: 10 minutes

Servings: 2

Nutritional Values

Calories 304

Total Fat 12 g

Saturated Fat 2.5 g

Cholesterol 0 mg

Sodium 5 mg

Total Carbs 47.9 g

Fiber 12.3 g

Sugar 25 g

Protein 3.7 g

Raspberry & Egg Smoothie

Ingredients

1 frozen banana, peeled and sliced

1½ cups fresh raspberries

2 eggs

1 tablespoon honey

½ cup plain yogurt

1 cup unsweetened almond milk

How to Prepare

1. Add all the ingredients in a high-power blender and pulse until creamy.

2. Pour the smoothie into two glasses and serve immediately.

Preparation time: 10 minutes

Total time: 10 minutes

Servings: 2

Nutritional Values

Calories 259

Total Fat 7.7 g

Saturated Fat 2.2 g

Cholesterol 167 mg

Sodium 196 mg

Total Carbs 38.8 g

Fiber 8.1 g

Sugar 24.6 g

Protein 11.3 g

Green Pumpkin Seed Smoothie

Ingredients

2 apples; peeled, cored, and chopped

1 cup frozen blueberries

2 cups fresh baby spinach

¼ cup pumpkin seeds

1½ tablespoons flax seeds

1 tablespoon raw wheat germ

4–6 drops liquid stevia

1½ cups fresh apple juice

How to Prepare

1. Add all the ingredients in a high-power blender and pulse until creamy.

2. Pour the smoothie into two glasses and serve immediately.

Preparation time: 10 minutes

Total time: 10 minutes

Servings: 2

Nutritional Values

Calories 384

Total Fat 10.9 g

Saturated Fat 1.9 g

Cholesterol 0 mg

Sodium 38 mg

Total Carbs 69.7 g

Fiber 10.8 g

Sugar 49.1 g

Protein 8.4 g

Lemony Blackberry Smoothie

Ingredients

2 cups frozen blackberries

1 small banana, peeled and sliced

2 tablespoons fresh lime juice

1 tablespoon honey

1 teaspoon lime zest, grated

½ cup plain yogurt

1 cup light coconut milk

How to Prepare

1. Add all the ingredients in a high-power blender and pulse until creamy.

2. Pour the smoothie into two glasses and serve immediately.

Preparation time: 10 minutes

Total time: 10 minutes

Servings: 2

Nutritional Values

Calories 259

Total Fat 7.6 g

Saturated Fat 5.2 g

Cholesterol 4 mg

Sodium 83 mg

Total Carbs 44.6 g

Fiber 9.1 g

Sugar 29.2 g

Protein 6.1 g

Cherry Smoothie

Ingredients

2 cup frozen cherries, pitted

1 medium frozen banana, peeled and sliced

1½ cups unsweetened almond milk

How to Prepare

1. Add all the ingredients in a high-power blender and pulse until creamy.

2. Pour the smoothie into two glasses and serve immediately.

Preparation time: 10 minutes

Total time: 10 minutes

Servings: 2

Nutritional Values

Calories 154

Total Fat 3.5 g

Saturated Fat 0.5 g

Cholesterol 0 mg

Sodium 137 mg

Total Carbs 32.1 g

Fiber 4.8 g

Sugar 21.2 g

Protein 2.8 g

Turmeric Fruity Smoothie

Ingredients

2 medium frozen bananas, peeled and sliced

1 cup frozen mango cubes

1 teaspoon fresh turmeric, peeled and grated

1 teaspoon fresh ginger, peeled and grated

1 tablespoon hemp seeds

¼ teaspoon vanilla extract

2 cups soy milk

How to Prepare

1. Add all the ingredients in a high-power blender and pulse until creamy.

2. Pour the smoothie into two glasses and serve immediately.

Preparation time: 10 minutes

Total time: 10 minutes

Servings: 2

Nutritional Values

Calories 316

Total Fat 6.9 g

Saturated Fat 0.9 g

Cholesterol 0 mg

Sodium 128 mg

Total Carbs 58.4 g

Fiber 6.3 g

Sugar 35.6 g

Protein 11.4 g